For Frank, SS
For Anna, SN

First published in Great Britain in 2001 by Zero To Ten Limited
327 High Street, Slough, Berkshire, SL1 1TX

Publisher: Anna McQuinn
Art Director: Tim Foster
Publishing Assistant: Vikram Parashar

A CIP catalogue record for this book is available from
the British Library.

ISBN 1-84089-145-9

Printed in Hong Kong

Let's look at
HANDS

Written by
Simona Sideri

Illustrated by
Sheilagh Noble

Look, hands are amazing!

How many fingers?

How many thumbs?

A mole's front paws have long broad nails...

that are
excellent for digging!

Bears have paws
with very long claws...

handy for hunting
and fetching food.

Seals use their flippers to swim,
like paddles.

On land their walk is more of a waddle.

Bats and birds
and other flying things
soar into the sky on their
wonderful wings.

Octopuses' tentacles
are long and thin.
They stretch them out
to bring prey in.

The suckers underneath
help them grip
onto rocks
and tightly stick.

Elephants use their trunks like hands!

Hands are **handy!**